Unwelcome Guests

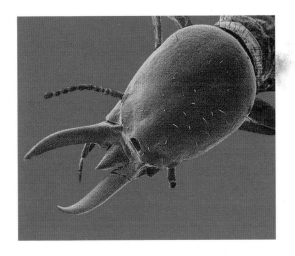

by Gary Miller

sundance™

A Haights Cross Communications ® Company

A Haights Cross Communications ◆® Company

Published by
Sundance Publishing
P.O. Box 740
One Beeman Road
Northborough, MA 01532-0740
800-343-8204
www.sundancepub.com

Unwelcome Guests
ISBN-13: 978-0-7608-9360-9
ISBN-10: 0-7608-9360-8

Illustrations by Tony Griego

Photo Credits
cover (background) ©Royalty-Free/CORBIS, (center) ©Jeff Rotman/Index Stock
Imagery; p. 1 ©Centre for Microscopy and Microanalysis, University of Queensland;
p. 6, 7 (spots) Scott Bauer/ARS/USDA; pp. 6–7 ©Robert Holmes/CORBIS; p. 7 (top)
©Centre for Microscopy and Microanalysis, University of Queensland; p. 8 (left)
©Michael Maconachie, Papilio/CORBIS, (center) Scott Camazine/Photo Researchers, Inc.,
(right) ©B. Borrell Casals, Frank Lane Picture Agency/CORBIS; p. 9 ©PREMAPHOTOS;
p. 10 (spot) Scott Bauer/ARS/USDA, (bottom) ©Philip Gould/CORBIS; p. 11 David
Nunuk/Science Photo Library; p. 14 ©W. Perry Conway/CORBIS; pp. 14–15 ©Gay
Bumgarner/Index Stock Imagery; p.16 ©Ray Bird, Frank Lane Picture Agency/CORBIS;
pp.18–19 Joe Raedle/Getty Images, Inc.; pp. 20–21 ©Layne Kennedy/CORBIS; p. 21
©Reuters/CORBIS; pp. 24–25 ©Jack Anthony; p. 27 USDA APHIS - Oxford, North
Carolina Archives, www.invasive.org; pp. 28–29 ©Eric Crichton/CORBIS; p. 29 ©John
T. Fowler; back cover (left) Scott Bauer/ARS/USDA, (right) ©W. Perry Conway/CORBIS

Printed in China

Table
of Contents

Who Invited Them?

Okay, it's time to go!

We said it's time to leave! But these animal guests won't go away easily. They're furry, slimy, and wiggly. You definitely don't want them around your house!

Toxic Hopper!

The giant toad is a giant pest in Florida. These big hoppers can be 9 inches long and weigh up to 2 pounds. They eat rats, mice, and small birds.

Giant toads are **native** to South and Central America. But they were released in Florida by accident in 1955. Now, many of them have moved into home gardens.

When they are scared, these toads give off a poison behind their head. The poison burns people's eyes. It can KILL dogs and cats!

Giant toad

This guy is in for a BIG surprise!

Giant toad: 9" long

Garden toad: 3" long

I wouldn't bite me if I were him.

Florida garden

They Came in Through the...Bathroom?

A rat can chew through walls to get to a tasty meal. A rat can even get into your house through your pipes!

1 Rat enters the sewer.

Hey, who are you calling a RAT?

Rats crawling through a drainpipe!

Rats live in **sewers** and are excellent swimmers. They can swim into drainpipes. These pipes may lead right into your bathroom. It's even easier for rats to get into bathrooms in basements!

What should you do if there's a rat swimming in your toilet? Close the lid and flush!

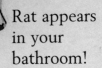

3 Rat appears in your bathroom!

2 Rat swims through drainpipes.

Alligators in the Toilet?

Are alligators living in New York sewers? Maybe not. Even though some New Yorkers flushed pet gators down toilets years ago, there is only one known case of a sewer gator. That gator escaped from a ship and swam into the sewer.

Gator Territory

One Wednesday evening, Jane Keefer of Sanibel, Florida, was gardening near her lakefront home. Suddenly, a 10-foot-long alligator grabbed her and dragged her into the lake! Fortunately, Ms. Keefer survived the attack.

Trapper removing alligator from pool

There are over 1 million alligators in Florida. As people move into the gators' habitats, they cross paths more often with the gators. During mating season, male alligators go on the move. They often show up on golf courses, in swimming pools—even in lakefront gardens!

Fishy Outlaw

The northern snakehead is a fishy fiend. Just a few of these **predators** will quickly gobble up all the other fish in a pond or lake.

This menace was brought to America from China by **aquarium** lovers. Other people brought it to raise for food. It soon got into the wild. That's been bad news for native fish.

Wildlife officials are trying to kill these fish. But snakeheads are tricky. They can live for days on land and even squirm to other ponds!

Where are all the fish?

WANTED DEAD

NOT ALIVE!

Small head, large mouth, big teeth, length up to 40 inches, and weight up to 15 pounds

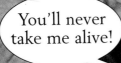

You'll never take me alive!

From Coast to Coast

So far, snakeheads have been found in these seven states.

Massachusetts
Maine
California
Rhode Island
Maryland
U.S.A.
Florida
Hawaii

Green Monsters

They're growing out of control. Somebody stop them!

Some plants cause plenty of problems. They can spread like crazy. They crowd out other plants. They can even hurt pets and people!

Vine of Doom!

How fast does kudzu grow? "Just plant it and run!" some people joke. Kudzu was brought to America in 1876 from Japan. People liked it and planted it for shade and as food for sheep and cows.

What happened? All I did was stop for lunch!

But soon the kudzu took over. It grew over other plants and trees, killing them. It covered houses, barns—even cars, buses, and trucks.

Today, kudzu covers over 7 million acres in the South!

Quack?

A nice kudzu dinner is one thing, but this is ridiculous!

Holy Cow!
If 7 million acres of kudzu were put together, they'd almost cover the state of Maryland!

A Wicked Weed

The giant hogweed looks pretty in gardens. That's why it was brought to America from Asia. But it soon started growing out of control!

This weed can grow taller than two men! Its leaves can be as much as five feet wide. Once it starts growing in a garden, it can take over.

But the worst thing about this weed is its **sap**. You don't want to touch it. The sap will send you to the hospital with a very nasty burn.

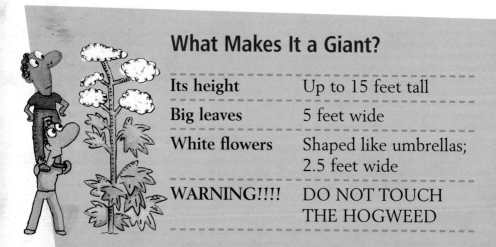

What Makes It a Giant?

Its height	Up to 15 feet tall
Big leaves	5 feet wide
White flowers	Shaped like umbrellas; 2.5 feet wide
WARNING!!!!	DO NOT TOUCH THE HOGWEED

Marsh Menace

Like the giant hogweed, the purple loosestrife is a pretty plant. But in wetlands across America, it's crowding out all the other plants.

I can't breathe!

Home Wrecker

Many plants, such as cattails, are used for food or in nest-making by wetland animals. Loosestrife crowds out these plants. Then animals lose their sources of food and shelter.

Beetle larvae eating loosestrife stem

In one national park, a few clumps of loosestrife grew out of control. In just a few years, this menace had covered nearly half of the park—1,600 acres!

People are fighting back with bugs that eat loosestrife. So far, these bugs seem to be making things better.

But will these bugs become unwelcome **guests,** too?

Fact File

Skunks are not only the stinkiest intruders, but they are also the biggest carriers of rabies.

Coyotes once lived mainly in the prairie. Today, coyotes can be found in most U.S. cities. So keep your pets inside, because coyotes like to eat them!

How did the giant-toad problem get to be so big? A female giant toad lays as many as 70,000 eggs a year!

Watch where you're going!

A cockroach will live for nine days without its head before it starves to death!